"WHO ARE YOU?"
Moses Asks God

Understanding God's Answer: Exodus 34:5–7

Joan Lipis

Foreword by Chad Holland

Printed in the U.S.A.
ISBN: 978-0-9978617-0-9
E-book ISBN: 978-0-9978617-1-6

Original cover artwork: Mary Jaracz
Cover photograph by Joan Lipis: Mt. Arbel, Galilee, Israel
Editorial services: Karen Roberts, RQuest, LLC
Interior formatting: Mary Jaracz

Contact the author at
Web: www.novea.org
Email: Novea@novea.org

NOVEA MINISTRIES

P.O. Box 62592
Colorado Springs, CO 80962

ENDORSEMENTS

With the awe and wonder of a child, Joanie searches the Scriptures to find treasures from heaven waiting for us to discover! Her passion for the God of Israel is as undeniable as it is contagious. How beautiful it is to walk through these pages, experience yourself in these stories, grab the richer meaning through Hebrew words, and discover things about the witness of Israel to the believer you never imagined.

Wendy K. Walters
President of The Favor Foundation • Motivational Speaker, Master Coach
www.wendykwalters.com

Who has never asked the question of God, "Who are You?" And who among us has never wondered, "Why am I here?" Grab a cup of coffee or tea, and pull up a chair at Joanie's table. Engage her in conversation by reading the wonderful insights into these questions, and you will be loved into the answers. For anyone who has realized that there is more to life than themselves, this is a must read. I needed two cups to savor the conversation.

Chuck Goldberg, MD
Physician, Surgeon, Wellness Coach
Sellwood Medical Center, Portland, OR

As I looked at the title of Joan's book, it invited me to read. Not only does this book enlighten, but it also encourages the reader's desire for a true relationship with the One God, creator of us all (Acts 17–26). It brings us upfront and personal with God. Joan's relationship with God the Father, Son, and Holy Spirit is lived in her own life. This new writing by her could be a how-to-book but instead it is a WHO I AM book because of the love she has freely received and responded to through her many challenges and experiences.

Dr. O. Virginia Phillips
President and Visionary • Women of Purpose, International
Tigard, Oregon

"WHO ARE YOU?"
Moses Asks God

Understanding God's Answer: Exodus 34:5–7

DEDICATION

For my cherished friends, beloved of God, both those
I've known and those I've not yet met, who are walking
through times of great pain and challenge.

I pray this little book will be an easy yet a profound read.

I pray for you, beloved reader, that as we walk together on this
journey, you will be encouraged. Our paths are different, but
our goal is the same: hearing God's answer to our question,

"God, who are You?"

This book is dedicated to Yeshua, my Savior, my Lord, my
life, my everything. May this effort bring Him glory.

*And the Word became flesh and dwelt among us, and
we beheld His glory, the glory as of the only begotten of
the Father, full of grace and truth.* (John 1:14)

*He is the image of the invisible God, the firstborn
over all creation.* (Colossians 1:15)

CONTENTS

FOREWORD

In the Bible, we see the apostle Paul live and minister with a sense of urgency. We can quickly get a deep sense that Joanie feels this same urgency in the Holy Spirit and wants people to know who God is. I believe God's heart for His creation is to actually know who He is, not just to know facts about Him. This book is a challenge to make sure that we view God in His rightful place as being the One who has the authority to ask us *why* we might do certain things, as opposed to our viewpoint that we have the authority to ask Him *why*. He does and allows certain things. The motivation for asking Him *why* evaporates in light of knowing WHO God is, as Joanie points out. Asking God *about* WHO He is, however, is a different story. God seems to enjoy this question, as He longs to reveal Himself to His creation.

I applaud Joanie for pulling the curtain of her life back and allowing us to connect with her examples and stories in order to better reveal who God is, what He has done, and what He desires to do in the future. As someone who uses personal stories in many of my sermons, teachings, and classes, I was refreshed by the presentation choice Joanie makes in mixing her topical points, Scripture passages, and personal stories all together. Pulling out the depth of meaning behind the original Hebrew words also adds to the richness of the truth that is being revealed.

Joanie gives significant time to explain that God is motivated to act in our best interest more out of WHO He is rather than who we are or what we have done, showing again Joanie's concentrated motive of desiring to reveal WHO God is to His creation. It is also clear that Joanie's Jewish heritage is important to her, as this dynamic shapes not only her experiences with God, but also her view and application of the Scriptures.

Chad Holland
Senior Pastor, King of Kings Community Jerusalem
CEO, King of Kings Ministries

PREFACE

Greetings and shalom from Jerusalem!

You have in your hand an explanation of the Hebrew words God uses to describe Himself to Moses. It also contains personal stories, jewels from my life, that illustrate and bring those words to life.

Knowing Hebrew isn't crucial to knowing God, but I believe that having even a slight familiarity with the words God uses will expand your understanding of who God is and increase your love for Him. Thus for each of the key words in God's self-revelation, I share both the denotation (definition) and connotation (subtle shades of meaning and uses) in the text.

So that I don't overwhelm you, I give the Hebrew font and English transliteration of Hebrew words sparingly. However, for your further understanding, I made bold the referenced words as they are used in specific passages. If you want to dig deeper, I encourage you to use my favorite resources listed in the back of this book.

I've also limited quoting Scripture to the barest minimum and footnoted related verses.

This book is for people who know Him, people who don't know Him, and even those who think they don't want to know Him. I hope that everyone who reads it will be blessed with a greater devotion and passion to know Him better.

As you read this, imagine we are in Jerusalem, sitting at an outdoor café. As we sip our tea and munch on a falafel, we swap stories about God.

I pray that you will savor my stories as much as the food and our fellowship.

God bless you, Beloved, with a greater knowledge, love, trust, and joy of Jesus (who I call Yeshua!).

Joanie

— 1 —

Questioning God

"Why?"

It's the all-important question, isn't it? Sooner or later, we all ask it.

I remember the day when I asked, no, I challenged God with my "Why?"

What about you?

How many times have you asked God that question? And when God is silent, how many times have you answered yourself? Or how many times have you asked someone else and then waited impatiently for an answer, only to be disappointed or confused by the answer?

Maybe you've searched through a myriad of books or listened to sermons that try to answer, "Why did God allow it?"

Well-meaning friends give unsatisfactory advice:

- "Just surrender."
- "Everything happens for a reason."
- "It must be God's will."
- "Just be patient, it'll be good in the end."

But somehow those answers are not enough.

You are not alone.

Job was a righteous man who loved God yet he asked, "Why?" Actually he challenged God to answer.

God responded, but not by answering Job's question. Instead He responded by questioning Job!

Job was silenced. He had no answer. In fact his questions paled, evaporated in God's presence.

Moses asked God a different question.

After God spoke to him through the burning bush and told him he was to lead Israel out of Egypt and into the Promised Land, Moses asked, "Who, me?"

> *But Moses said to God, "Who am I that I should go to Pharaoh, and that I should bring the children of Israel out of Egypt?"* (Exodus 3:11)

Beloved, "but" is not the best way to start a conversation with God!

God's answer, a reassurance to go with him, wasn't satisfactory to Moses, so he changed his question.

> *Then Moses said to God, "Indeed, when I come to the children of Israel and say to them, 'The God of your fathers has sent me to you,' and they say to me, 'What is His name?' what shall I say to them?"* (Exodus 3:13)

"Who are You?" Moses asked God.

Jesus' disciples asked the same question, more to themselves than to Jesus (Mark 4:41). Knowing the people had been asking that same question among themselves, Jesus asked His disciples:

> *Who do men say that I am?* (Mark 8:27)

The answer for Job, Moses, the disciples, Israel, and you, Beloved, is found in God's name.

— 2 —
The Context
Exodus 2:23–25

What's in a name? To the Hebrew people, a person's name is intrinsically related to his/her character. It is the reason God often changes people's names or tells parents what to name their children. [1]

Scripture tells us that Abraham knew God as "God Almighty" (Genesis 6:2–3). But many years later, God revealed His memorial name to Moses.

> *God said to Moses, "I AM WHO I AM." And He said, "Thus you shall say to the children of Israel, 'I AM has sent me to you.'" Moreover God said to Moses, "Thus you shall say to the children of Israel: 'The LORD God of your fathers, the God of Abraham, the God of Isaac, and the God of Jacob, has sent me to you. This is My name forever, and this is My memorial to all generations.'"* (Exodus 3:14–15)

To this day arguments abound about how to pronounce God's name. Many Jews feel the name is too holy to write or to speak, so they omit a letter when writing ("L-rd" or "G-d") and say "Adonai" in their prayers. Or they might simply say, "*HaShem*," meaning "The Name."

Then there are those who use the Hebrew letters, translated into English as YHWH. Still others just say, "I AM." [2]

Regardless of how we say His name, what's really important is that we know what it means.

To understand God's memorial name, we need to understand the larger context in which God revealed it.

Israel was in bondage in Egypt and God was about to deliver her. Israel's deliverance on the night of the Passover is such a crucial part of the identity and culture of Israel that it is still commemorated and celebrated today.

The story opens with Jacob's family living in Egypt. Life was easy…but only for a while.

There arose a new king over Egypt, who did not know Joseph. (Exodus 1:8)

Pharaoh, afraid of Israel's increasing population, put the Jews into bitter and cruel slavery. The situation seemed hopeless. The people felt rejected, abandoned, and betrayed by God.

They had heard stories about Abraham, the great man of faith. They had heard how God had commanded him to sacrifice his son Isaac. Perhaps the children held their breath waiting to hear what would happen. Maybe they cheered when God sent a ram as the substitute sacrifice.

They had heard the amazing stories about Abraham's offspring: Isaac, Jacob, and Joseph. They remembered God's promise to bring them into their own land, a land where they would be free.

But after so many years in slavery, eventually hope in God's promise faded.

Now it happened in the process of time that the king of Egypt died. Then the children of Israel groaned because of the bondage, and they cried out; and their cry came up to God because of the bondage. (Exodus 2:23)

As the bondage in Egypt grew worse, questions replaced hope.

- "Where is God?"
- "Has He forgotten us?"
- "What about His promises?"
- "Does He know what's happening?"
- "Does He see?"
- "Does He care?"

And the persistent but unanswerable, "WHY?"

Praying was impossible. Israel groaned.

But God was neither blind nor deaf.

> *So God heard their groaning, and God remembered His covenant with Abraham, with Isaac, and with Jacob. And God looked upon the children of Israel, and God acknowledged them.* (Exodus 2:24–25)

God hadn't forgotten His promises. Not only did He hear, but He also looked upon their grief and understood. And at just the right time, He began to fulfill His promises to Israel.

The four Hebrew action verbs used in this passage have great significance in our understanding of who God is.

God *heard* their groaning.

The Hebrew root שָׁמַע [*shama*ʿ] means *to listen with interest, attentively, often leading to obedience.* [3]

The word appears again in Deuteronomy 6:4, which is recited throughout the world in Jewish and Messianic communities.

> **Hear,** *O Israel: The LORD our God, the LORD is one!* (Deuteronomy 6:4)

This verse is spoken as a prayer and as a declaration of faith. Yet because the first word is *shamaʿ*, I suggest it is more of a command than a prayer, a command to hear and to obey.

Joanie's Jewel

I think we've all been in a similar situation as Israel, when we couldn't pray but could only groan.

I have. I remember times when I was too discouraged, too tired, too confused, or in too much pain to do anything else but groan. Here's one such time.

I had recently moved to Israel and knew only a few people. One night I suffered a flare up of a chronic illness and needed medication immediately. I knew what I needed but had neither a doctor nor a prescription.

A friend drove me to the nearest emergency room but then left for a previous appointment. I couldn't speak Hebrew, and the nurses couldn't speak English.

I felt very alone.

Finally I was examined and then left alone again. Time dragged by. Minutes became hours. My spirit groaned within me. Finally a nurse returned but we couldn't understand each other. So I pointed to my watch and shrugged as if to say, "What's taking so long?"

The nurse had a one-word response: "Cancer."

Apparently they were checking to see if I had cancer. How or why I didn't know, and the nurse didn't explain.

I was alone again, but now my mind kept repeating that word over and over. Then I smiled even as tears trickled down my face. *Why am I smiling?* I wondered.

The realization hit like a wall crashing over me. I was tired of the battle of life. I was tired of the pain of my past and the confusion and the challenges of moving halfway across the world—alone. The thought of dying of cancer was not frightening or painful in that moment. I wanted to go to my heavenly home.

Even so, God had *heard* my groaning. Quietly and gently, He spoke to my innermost being.

"You've known Me as your King. Now know Me as your Good Shepherd."

What happened next?

There was no cancer. I received the needed medicine, and today my Good Shepherd has completely healed me!

God *remembered* His covenant.

God does not forget. While we don't understand and usually don't like His timing, He remembers His promises. He knew when it was time to fulfill His covenant promises to His people in bondage, and He knows when it is time to fulfill His promises to each of us.

Listen to Israel's worship and prayers and you can hear how they are based on God's covenant promises. [4]

> *Then Solomon stood before the altar of the LORD in the presence of all the assembly of Israel, and spread out his hands toward heaven; and he said: "LORD God of Israel, there is no God in heaven above or on earth below like You, who keep Your covenant and mercy with Your servants who walk before You with all their hearts. You have kept what You promised Your servant David my father; You have*

both spoken with Your mouth and fulfilled it with Your hand, as it is this day." (1 Kings 8:22–24)

Likewise for us, there is no stronger foundation for our prayer and praise than the promises in God's written, revealed Word. He does not forget His promises to us.

Joanie's Jewel

Before my move to Israel in 1986, my first major move was from the East to the West Coast. The emotional pain of the previous thirty-five-plus years had become too heavy. I reasoned that if I could just move away, I could leave behind the weight of the rejection, abandonment, and betrayal.

Somehow the pain came with me.

Despite my new location I continued to suffer. It wasn't long before I found myself standing in front of a hospital door that said "Mental Health Ward."

The long-term use of steroids for the chronic illness had intensified my emotional issues to the point that doctors decided they had to get me off the medicine quickly. The hospital was the best place, they said. Today I agree that it was the right decision, but at the time I was furious.

The hospital was surrounded by hills. One day as I looked at those hills I remembered Psalm 121. With clenched teeth and a raised fist, I challenged God. "You said, *'He who keeps Israel never slumbers nor sleeps.'* Well, I'm Israel. I'm here. Why? Where are You?"

God started answering that challenge immediately. My anger began the process of releasing the emotional pain. Over the next few weeks, I discovered many truths about my past and myself.

The healing had begun.

My prayer, or more accurately my challenge to God, was based on His covenant promise to Israel.

God *looked* upon the children.

The Hebrew root רָאָה [*ra'ah*] means much more than simply to see or to look at. It means *to inspect, perceive, consider.*[5]

In other words, it means *to see in a way that goes beyond the visual.* If God knows even the number of hairs on our heads (Matthew 10:30), is there anything in our lives He cannot or does not see and respond to?

A derivative form of the word means *to provide* as we can see by these two wonderful stories.

When Sarah (Abraham's wife) began to treat Hagar (Abraham's concubine) badly, Hagar took her son Ishmael and ran away. I'm sure Hagar felt abandoned, betrayed, and very much alone. But God saw her. Scripture says the "Angel of the LORD" found her and gave her instructions and hope.[6]

In her response, we find the Hebrew word for *look* and a derivative used three times in one verse.

> Then she called the name of the LORD *who spoke to her, You-Are-the-God-Who-***Sees***; for she said, "Have I also here* **seen** *Him who* **sees** *me?"* (Genesis 16:13)

In the story of Abraham offering Isaac as a sacrifice, we hear this same word and a derivative.

> And Abraham said, "My son, God will **provide** *for Himself the lamb for a burnt offering." So the two of them went together…Then Abraham*

lifted his eyes and **looked**, *and there behind him was a ram caught in a thicket by its horns. So Abraham went and took the ram, and offered it up for a burnt offering instead of his son. And Abraham called the name of the place, The-*LORD*-Will-***Provide***; as it is said to this day, "In the Mount of the* LORD *it shall be* ***provided***.*" (Genesis 22:8,13–14)

Beloved, in this passage the same Hebrew word is used for *look* and *provide!* God not only sees and perceives, but He also provides what is needed in our situations.

Joanie's Jewel

God has surprised me so many times as He sees and provides not only for my "need" but often for my "want." I don't just mean the way He provides financially, physically, or emotionally. One time He provided in a very practical way as I attempted to do something I'm not equipped to do. Let me start from the beginning.

I am a visionary and not an administrator, but I didn't realize the difference until overwhelming stress and confusion brought the project to a standstill.

Wanting to hide, I visited a church where I thought no one knew me. But when the usher walked me to a seat, the woman in the next seat looked up in astonishment. With the blood draining from her face, she could only say, "It's you!"

As I sat down, she continued. "I've been seeing your face in my thoughts for days. Do you have a need?"

"Yes!" I practically shouted. "I am desperate for someone who is good at administration. But who are you?"

Well, you might guess the rest of the story. Maggie had seen me while at her job as a receptionist for the local Christian television station, where I had visited. She was an excellent administrator. The project moved forward and was completed under our partnership, to the glory of God and the salvation of a precious Jewish man. [7]

God *acknowledged* them.

This word is one of my favorites. The Hebrew יָדַע [*yada*] means *to know by experience, to recognize, admit, acknowledge, and confess.* [8] It is the kind of "knowing" that comes from the intimacy between a husband and wife.

Scripture says God knows us that intimately. Consider Psalm 139:1–6.

> *O Lord, You have searched me and* **known** *me.*
> *You* **know** *my sitting down and my rising up;*
> *You understand my thought afar off.*
> *You comprehend my path and my lying down,*
> *And are acquainted with all my ways.*
> *For there is not a word on my tongue,*
> *But behold, O Lord, You* **know** *it altogether.*
> *You have hedged me behind and before,*
> *And laid Your hand upon me.*
> *Such* **knowledge** *is too wonderful for me;*
> *It is high, I cannot attain it.*

As the Father knows us intimately so does Jesus, God the Son. The writer of the book of Hebrews recorded,

> *For we do not have a High Priest who cannot sympathize with our weaknesses.* (Hebrews 4:15)

Joanie's Jewel

Growing up in a Jewish home, I was not unfamiliar with the name of Jesus; I knew He was crucified. After all, I had seen pictures of the crucifixion, and some of my friends wore crosses. But I didn't know much about Him. I had no answers to these two very important questions:

- *Who* was He?
- *Why* was He crucified?

I believed that Jesus had no significance to the Jewish people other than the fact that He was one.

Sadly what I did know was that in the name of Jesus, many Jews were hated, persecuted, and even killed.

But one day all that changed as I watched a sculptor molding clay into the bust of a man. The words of Isaiah 53 were read in the background.

> *Who has believed our report?*
> *And to whom has the arm of the LORD been revealed?*
> *For He shall grow up before Him as a tender plant,*
> *And as a root out of dry ground.*
> *He has no form or comeliness;*
> *And when we see Him,*
> *There is no beauty that we should desire Him.* (Isaiah 53:1–2)

I was mesmerized. Instinctively I knew these words had something to do with Jesus.

> *He is despised and rejected by men,*
> *A Man of sorrows and acquainted with grief.*
> *And we hid, as it were, our faces from Him;*
> *He was despised, and we did not esteem Him.* (Isaiah 53:3)

I was seeing a different Jesus. Suddenly I was confronted by the reality of the pain Jesus had experienced. I'd never considered all the pain Jesus had suffered both physically and emotionally.

He had experienced the pain of rejection, abandonment, and betrayal. He understood *my* pain; He could sympathize with *my* weaknesses.

Then to my astonishment came these words:

> *Surely He has borne our griefs*
> *And carried our sorrows;*
> *Yet we esteemed Him stricken,*
> *Smitten by God, and afflicted.*
>
> *But He was wounded for our transgressions,*
> *He was bruised for our iniquities;*
> *The chastisement for our peace was upon Him,*
> *And by His stripes we are healed.* (Isaiah 53:4–5)

This Jesus was not the one that I thought I knew. This Jesus suffered such horrendous pain. And this Jesus suffered all that pain—**for me!**

While that realization didn't answer all of my questions, it was sufficient to challenge me to respond. If *that* Jesus knew me, I wanted to know Him. [9]

Beloved, when I'm facing a situation that tempts me to doubt God's concern for me, feeling discouraged, ignored, or misunderstood, I hang onto the truth that He does understand, He does care, and He will act when and how it will be best for me. I hang onto the truth that not only will it be best for me, but also whatever He does will bring Him glory.

God *Acts*

God seeing, hearing, and knowing Israel's oppression and sorrow wouldn't have been enough. God *had* to act. It is an essential aspect of His character.

> *And the LORD said: "I have surely seen the oppression of My people who are in Egypt, and have heard their cry because of their taskmasters, for I know their sorrows. So..."* (Exodus 3:7–8a)

The little word *so* here is tremendously important to understand God's memorial name and His character. Now read the rest of the sentence.

> *"...I have come down to deliver them out of the hand of the Egyptians, and to bring them up from that land to a good and large land.* (Exodus 3:8)

God heard, remembered, saw, and understood Israel's trouble, *SO* He came down to deliver, redeem, and rescue her.

God's deliverance of Israel was based on His unique covenant relationship with her. The entire Passover event was the platform through which God revealed to the world who He is.

So that the people would never forget, God often referred to Himself as the "God who brought you out of Egypt."

One well-known example is found in the book of Samuel.

> *Then Samuel called the people together to the LORD at Mizpah, and said to the children of Israel, "Thus says the LORD God of Israel: 'I brought up Israel out of Egypt, and delivered you from the hand of the Egyptians and from the hand of all kingdoms and from those who oppressed you.'"* (1 Samuel 10:17–18) [10]

There are seven Psalms that are traditionally sung at Passover celebrations: Psalms 113–118 and Psalm 136. These Psalms, known as the Great Hallel, conjoin God's character and His actions.

> *Who is like the LORD our God,*
> *Who dwells on high,*
> *Who humbles Himself to behold*
> *The things that are in the heavens and in the earth?*
> *He raises the poor out of the dust,*
> *And lifts the needy out of the ash heap,*
> *That He may seat him with princes—*
> *With the princes of His people.* (Psalm 113:5–8) [11]

Israel was in trouble and God acted.

If Scripture can be likened to a symphony, this refrain would be heard from beginning to end:

- Man is in trouble
  - Man cries to God
- God hears
  - God acts to deliver

Beloved, doesn't what God did for Israel sound similar to what God did several thousand years later not only for Israel but for the world? [12]

> *For God so loved the world that He gave His only begotten Son, that whoever believes in Him should not perish but have everlasting life. For God did not send His Son into the world to condemn the world, but that the world through Him might be saved.* (John 3:16–17)

Joanie's Jewel

In the heart of Jerusalem there is a garden that many people believe is the actual burial place of Jesus. Right beyond its fence is a rock formation that looks like a skull, lending credibility to its claim of being Golgotha. I often go there to meditate and reflect on the wonder of God's love.

One day, a young woman sat nearby; often people weep in the garden, but her tears seemed different. She was greatly distressed. Apologetically, Dana poured out her complaint: "I just cannot believe God loves me. I keep asking Him to prove His love to me, but He is so silent."

How well I understood that sense of frustration, knowing God hears and understands but being unable to hear His voice, see His salvation, or feel His love.

I have found the best way to remember God's love is to journey to Golgotha. Come with me. We will start at the top of the Mount of Olives. From that hill, God's plan from eternity past until eternity future coalesced in twenty-four hours.

Take a few moments to look at Jerusalem. Look through the eyes of Jesus as He takes one final look at His beloved city. Let your heart break, as His breaks, with love for the people as well as for the city. Look with Him at the city where He has chosen to put His name. Look at the temple with all its ritual sacrifices. See the smoke rising up from the burnt offerings and the altar of incense, filling the city with a sweet but pungent fragrance. Remember the sacrifice Abraham was willing to make. Then consider what may be in the heart of Jesus in knowing that He, the spotless Lamb, is about to be sacrificed by the very people He came to save.

Allow tears to flow down your cheeks; you are crying as He did, tears of passion and compassion.

We continue down—always toward Gethsemane.

Here's the place where Jesus was scourged. Count the strokes: one… two…three–thirty-nine in all. His flesh is being ripped apart; the crown of thorns is piercing His scalp.

We join the crowds working our way along the Via Dolorosa. People are pushing, shoving, and crushing us as they try to get a better look.

The noise is deafening. The soldiers are shouting at the people, "Get away! Move back! Make room!"

Jesus stumbles under the weight of the cross.

People are jeering, spitting, or mocking Him. Some are laughing. But some are crying.

We've reached Golgotha. Stop!

Remember the words of Isaiah.

> *He was oppressed and He was afflicted,*
> *Yet He opened not His mouth;*
> *He was led as a lamb to the slaughter,*
> *And as a sheep before its shearers is silent,*
> *So He opened not His mouth.*
> *He was taken from prison and from judgment,*
> *And who will declare His generation?*
> *For He was cut off from the land of the living;*
> *For the transgressions of My people He was stricken.*
> *And they made His grave with the wicked–*
> *But with the rich at His death,*
> *Because He had done no violence,*
> *Nor was any deceit in His mouth.*

Yet it pleased the LORD *to bruise Him;*
He has put Him to grief. (Isaiah 53:7–10a)

Take a long look at Golgotha:

See from His head, His hands, His feet,
Sorrow and love flow mingling down;
Did e'er such love and sorrow meet,
Or thorns compose so rich a crown? [13]

Sorrow. Not shame, but sorrow. Not anger or fear, but sorrow. Sorrow for those who refuse and reject His love, the love manifested through Jesus on the Cross. [14]

We considered that God understands our feelings but can we comprehend His? Read again the description of the torture and try to understand God's feelings. I'm sure that "pleasure" was not on your list. And yet, the prophet said that "it pleased the LORD to bruise Him," that I AM was ultimately responsible for the crucifixion.

Why?

Because of who God is!

Precious friend, I pray you will realize as I have, that "I AM" is actively and intimately involved in every part of your life. He hears your groans, remembers His promises to you, sees and understands your deepest feelings, and acts to deliver you.

Now, finish your journey at the empty tomb!

— 3 —

Moses Asks God

What a privilege God gave to Moses! God revealed His love and His plan to rescue Israel and then to bring her into the Promised Land.

But even after leading Israel out of Egypt, Moses was still not satisfied with his knowledge and understanding of who God is.

Despite all he had already heard from God and seen Him do for Israel, Moses was not ready to accept the next part of God's assignment. Personally, I think Moses was terrified because it was such a daunting assignment. Why else would he have had the nerve to keep questioning God?

Moses required much more from God. You've got to admit, Moses had "chutzpah" (Jewish nerve)!

> *Then Moses said to the LORD, "See, You say to me, 'Bring up this people.' But You have not let me know whom You will send with me. Yet You have said, 'I know you by name, and you have also found grace in My sight.' Now therefore, I pray, if I have found grace in Your sight, show me now Your way, that I may know You and that I may find grace in Your sight. And consider that this nation is Your people."*
>
> *And He said, "My Presence will go with you, and I will give you rest."*
>
> *Then he said to Him, "If Your Presence does not go with us, do not bring us up from here. For how then will it be known that Your people*

and I have found grace in Your sight, except You go with us? So we shall be separate, Your people and I, from all the people who are upon the face of the earth."

So the LORD said to Moses, "I will also do this thing that you have spoken; for you have found grace in My sight, and I know you by name." (Exodus 33:12–17)

Amazingly, God wasn't angry with Moses for questioning and challenging Him. Instead He was moved by Moses' request. He responded by promising Moses that His presence would go with him.

Yet even the promise of God's presence wasn't enough. Moses asked for more.

And he said, "Please, show me Your glory." (Exodus 33:18)

Basically Moses was asking again the question that has echoed down through the centuries:

"Who *are* You?"

How would you answer that question if someone you just met asked you? Would you be humble and demure, giving only bits of yourself? Would you be proud and boast of all your accomplishments? For sure, you probably would leave lots unsaid.

But God *wants* to be known, loved, and trusted.

King David understood.

And those who know Your name will put their trust in You. (Psalm 9:10a)

So when Moses asked for more, God responded.

Then He said, "I will make all My goodness pass before you, and I will proclaim the name of the LORD before you." (Exodus 33:19a)

Joanie's Jewel

God was about to reveal His glory to Moses.

If this story were to be made into a movie, there would now be a drum roll or maybe an absolute angelic hush.

I cannot imagine how Moses might have felt when God summoned him up Mount Sinai. I remember how I felt when I went to the House of Lords in London.

Being an American, I really didn't understand or appreciate royalty or such traditions which seemed to be pompous and showy.

I had to stand in complete silence as the Lords walked into their chamber. Down the hall they came, dressed in their black gowns and white, powdered wigs. But as they passed, I was caught up in the moment and wondered if I should bow or courtesy.

Then I went into the chamber itself. The mahogany wood was polished to a shine. It was breathtaking.

But everything I had seen so far faded when I saw the throne at the center of the massive room. Although it wasn't the official throne used at state affairs, it still commanded my attention.

I'm sure this throne doesn't compare to what awaits us in the Throne Room of God!

— 4 —

God Answers Moses

Who God is, or His character, is the foundation for what He does. And while it doesn't answer the fundamental question of *why* He does what He does, that question seems to evaporate in light of knowing *who* God is.

So let's hear God's answer to Moses as recorded in Exodus 34:5–7.

We're going to look at the passage in two parts. The Hebrew words God uses to describe Himself in the first part (6–7a) are found in many other places in Scripture with only slight variations. [15]

But we won't stop at verse 7a. There's more, so continue with me to the second part and on to the end!

In the second part (Exodus 34:7b) we'll look at four aspects of His forgiving nature.

From beginning to end, each word God uses to describe Himself is like a facet of a precious jewel, each one a revelation of His glory.

Moses was about to see and hear from God in a way that no mortal before or after him ever experienced.

Exodus 34:6–7a

Before God would reveal more of His name and His character to Moses on Mount Sinai, He instructed Moses to prepare for their meeting.

> And the LORD said to Moses, "Cut two tablets of stone like the first ones, and I will write on these tablets the words that were on the first tablets which you broke. So be ready in the morning, and come up in the morning to Mount Sinai, and present yourself to Me there on the top of the mountain. And no man shall come up with you, and let no man be seen throughout all the mountain; let neither flocks nor herds feed before that mountain."
>
> So he cut two tablets of stone like the first ones. Then Moses rose early in the morning and went up Mount Sinai, as the LORD had commanded him; and he took in his hand the two tablets of stone.
>
> Now the LORD descended in the cloud and stood with him there, and proclaimed the name of the LORD. (Exodus 34:1–5)

Now let's join Moses at Mount Sinai as God reveals Himself to Moses (and to us).

> Now the LORD descended in the cloud and stood with him there, and proclaimed the name of the LORD. And the LORD passed before him and proclaimed, "The LORD, the LORD God, **merciful** and **gracious**, **longsuffering**, and abounding in **goodness** and **truth**, keeping **mercy** for thousands." (Exodus 34:5–7a, emphases mine)

Merciful

What is the first word you would use to describe God?

The very first word God uses to describe Himself in this passage is translated as "merciful." Sadly the English doesn't express the depth of the word's meaning.

The Hebrew רַחוּם [*rachum*] comes from the root רָחַם [*racham*] and refers to a *deep love (usually of a superior for an inferior) rooted in some natural bond.* [16] "It expresses intensive or intentional and repeated action. It is also the root for 'womb,' thus reflecting the deep feeling people have toward babies or helpless animals." [17]

I'm going to get a little technical here. The New King James Bible uses "mercy" or "merciful" about 300 times, but the Hebrew root, *racham* is used only 35 times. Recognizing where this word is used and understanding its depth brings a greater appreciation of who God is. Most of the uses of "mercy" or "merciful" are actually the Hebrew word *hesed*. (see page 31)

Joanie's Jewel

I've never had a child, but when parents talk about the first time they see their newborn, they struggle for words. They use words like, "incredible, unbelievable, life-changing." The closest I can come is holding a newborn puppy!

Well what they were feeling is *racham*, the overwhelming love that comes from the very depths of being. Beloved, this is the first word God used to describe Himself! He loves you with that kind of love.

I came close to understanding that kind of love when I was taking care of the young daughter of a friend. Kirstie was about two years old and extremely active. Getting her to take a nap necessitated great creativity.

Her parents had discovered a secret weapon—the car. Put Kirstie into a car seat, and she would be asleep within seconds. We drove many miles that week!

One day in particular had been rather stressful. She was into everything, and my patience was wearing thin. "To the car," I suggested. "Let's have an adventure!" Of course, by the time we arrived at the promised little creek, she was sleeping soundly.

I parked the car and watched her. Her eyes were shut tight, but there was a smile on her lips. Her face was serene and practically glowed with an innocence that belied her actions earlier in the day.

As I watched her, my heart began to swell with love. Love grew and grew until my heart ached. I thought it would burst into a thousand pieces. Gone was the frustration of the morning. Gone was my impatience. There was only a rising sense of contentment and joy. Nothing could mar or stain the moment.

She looked so fragile. For a few more days she'd be dependent on me. Feelings previously unknown rose up from the very core of my being. I wanted to defend, protect, and provide for her needs. I wanted to nurture and nourish her in the love of God and then stand back and watch her blossom into the flower He created her to be.

Suddenly it occurred to me that my love for this child was based on absolutely nothing. She wasn't my flesh and blood. She wasn't *doing* anything to win my approval. Although she was a precious child, bright, attentive, loving, and kind, none of those qualities were the reasons I loved her. I loved her because I loved her! In that moment, I caught a glimpse of how God feels about us.

Beloved, God loves us not because of anything we do or not do, but because of who He *is*. His *rachum*, or compassionate love, rises up from the depth of His being. It is the first word He uses to describe Himself to Moses.

Gracious

The second word God uses to describe Himself is translated as *gracious*.

The Hebrew חַנּוּן [*chanun*] comes from the root חָנַן [*chanan*], which means *to be gracious, show favor, pity, seek, or implore favor.* [18] *Chanan* "denotes the stronger coming to the help of the weaker who stands in need of help by reason of his circumstances or natural weakness. He acts by a voluntary decision, though he is moved by the dependence or the request of the weaker party. The action itself is what makes the weaker party acceptable." [19]

This same word is used repeatedly in Exodus 33:12–17 as God assured Moses that he had found grace in His eyes.

> *Then Moses said to the LORD, "See, You say to me, 'Bring up this people.' But You have not let me know whom You will send with me. Yet You have said, 'I know you by name, and you have also found **grace** in My sight.' Now therefore, I pray, if I have found **grace** in Your sight, show me now Your way, that I may know You and that I may find **grace** in Your sight. And consider that this nation is Your people." And He said, "My Presence will go with you, and I will give you rest."*
>
> *Then he said to Him, "If Your Presence does not go with us, do not bring us up from here. For how then will it be known that Your people and I have found **grace** in Your sight, except You go with us? So we shall be separate, Your people and I, from all the people who are upon the face of the earth."*
>
> *So the LORD said to Moses, "I will also do this thing that you have spoken; for you have found grace in My sight, and I know you by name." (Exodus 33:12–17)*

Joanie's Jewel

God's grace can be seen most clearly when we recognize our almost helpless state. As I have learned, we dare not take for granted even our ability to breathe.

The reality of my dependence on God's grace confronted me while swimming in the Mediterranean Sea. Foolishly, and like many others, I ignored the black flags warning swimmers to stay out of the water. Jumping the waves and standing against the undertow was fun for a while. Suddenly I was carried farther and farther out to sea. I was held powerless in the grip of the water.

I had no time to panic; I had to pray. God's grace came in the shape of three powerful swimmers who were able to push and pull me out of the water.

As God's grace was there for Israel and me in our times of need, He is there for you. Beloved, one cry from you, and He is ready to come to your rescue. He has committed the life of His Son to love, protect, and provide for you.

To what extent, you may wonder? The apostle Paul tells us God committed the life of His Son to love, protect, and provide for us.

> *For when we were still without strength, in due time Christ died for the ungodly. For scarcely for a righteous man will one die; yet perhaps for a good man someone would even dare to die. But God demonstrates His own love toward us, in that while we were still sinners, Christ died for us.* (Romans 5:6–8)

We are all caught in the grip of powerful forces of darkness and sin and are in desperate need. Only God can and will satisfy our need. His grace toward His created ones is part of His character, His nature, His name.

Longsuffering

The third word God uses to describe Himself is actually two Hebrew words, translated together as "longsuffering," אֶרֶךְ אַף. The Hebrew root אָרֵךְ ['arek] "is used to express the Lord's attitude of anger toward the covenant people when they have sinned." The derivative used here, אַף ['af], refers to the nose and, by extension, to the face. [20]

Imagine someone who is so angry his nose gets red and his nostrils flare. An angry horse is a great example too. When aroused to anger, its nostrils appear quite large and flared.

King David used that picture of flaring nostrils of a horse to describe God's anger.

> *In my distress I called upon the LORD,*
> *And cried out to my God;*
> *He heard my voice from His temple,*
> *And my cry came before Him, even to His ears.*
> *Then the earth shook and trembled;*
> *The foundations of the hills also quaked and were shaken,*
> *Because He was angry.*
> *Smoke went up from His nostrils,*
> *And devouring fire from His mouth;*
> *Coals were kindled by it.* (Psalm 18:6–8)

God's face is extremely important in the Hebrew Bible as a symbol or sign of His favor. When God's face (countenance) looks upon His children, His blessings follow.

> *For they did not gain possession of the land by their own sword,*
> *Nor did their own arm save them;*
> *But it was Your right hand, Your arm, and the light of Your countenance,*
> *Because You favored them.* (Psalm 44:3)

God commanded Aaron to put this "face blessing" upon the people of Israel:

> And the LORD spoke to Moses, saying: "Speak to Aaron and his sons, saying, 'This is the way you shall bless the children of Israel. Say to them:
>
> > "The LORD bless you and keep you;
> > The LORD make His face shine upon you, And be gracious to you;
> > The LORD lift up His countenance upon you, and give you peace.'"
>
> "So they shall put My name on the children of Israel, and I will bless them." (Numbers 6:22–27)

Joanie's Jewel

Lovers can bear to be separated, but not to be rejected. Great is the pain when a lover turns away, refusing to show his or her face to the beloved. Imagine the horror of God turning His face away. From the deepest part of his heart, the psalmist cried:

> How long, O LORD? Will You forget me forever?
> How long will You hide Your face from me?
> How long shall I take counsel in my soul,
> Having sorrow in my heart daily? (Psalm 13:1–2a)

God must turn His face away when His children sin.

> Behold, the LORD's hand is not shortened,
> That it cannot save;
> Nor His ear heavy,
> That it cannot hear.
> But your iniquities have separated you from your God;
> And your sins have hidden His face from you,
> So that He will not hear. (Isaiah 59:1–2)

The good news is that in His patient, longsuffering nature, God allows time us to repent.

> For He has not despised nor abhorred the affliction of the afflicted;
> Nor has He hidden His face from Him;
> But when He cried to Him, He heard. (Psalm 22:24)

When the time was right, God the Father made provision through Jesus, God the Son, for our sins to be forgiven so that He can turn His face back toward His beloved when they acknowledge Him.

> God set forth [Jesus] as a propitiation by His blood, through faith, to demonstrate His righteousness, because in His forbearance God had passed over the sins that were previously committed, to demonstrate at the present time His righteousness, that He might be just and the justifier of the one who has faith in Jesus. (Romans 3:25–26)

Goodness and Truth

Next God used this two-word phrase that is often used throughout Scripture. To better understand the depth of the meaning of these words, let's first consider them separately.

Goodness

Without doubt, I can say that my favorite Hebrew word in Scripture is חֶסֶד [hesed], which is usually translated as *lovingkindness, mercy, and goodness.* However, none of these translations adequately captures the word's depth and breadth. Even Hebrew lexicons have difficulty in defining this incredible word. In my opinion, the best definition is *faithful, covenant-keeping love.*

While *hesed* is most often used in reference to God, the word is sometimes used in relationships between people. A beautiful example is in the story of Ruth, where English translations use *kindness*.

> *And Naomi said to her two daughters-in-law, "Go, return each to her mothers' house. The LORD deal* **kindly** *with you, as you have dealt with the dead and with me."* (Ruth 1:8) [21]

This word also reflects God's passionate (bridal) love for us, as can be seen in the story of Esther.

> *The king loved Esther more than all the other women, and she obtained grace and* **favor** *in his sight more than all the virgins; so he set the royal crown upon her head and made her queen instead of Vashti.* (Esther 2:17) [22]

The word *hesed* is best seen, however, in God's covenant relationship with Israel.

"I AM" bound Himself in covenant relationship with Abraham, Isaac, and Jacob, despite knowing the faithlessness of the people who were "in their loins!" It was an unconditional, eternal, and everlasting covenant relationship that God would not, could not, will not break. [23]

God is forever loyal to His word, which is based on His character. While the Mosaic Covenant was conditioned upon Israel's obedience (Deuteronomy 30), the Abrahamic Covenant and the New Covenant are unconditional, totally based on God's covenant-keeping love for His people.

God chose Israel to be His witness to the world. Through Israel, (the people, the nation, and the land), He would reveal His character, His power, and especially His covenant-keeping love.

Therefore, understanding the depth of God's *hesed* is impacted by understanding the covenant He made to Abraham (Genesis 12:1–3, 7).

Unlike the New Covenant wherein individuals choose to accept the covenant, God chose Israel for His purposes.

God's *hesed* isn't influenced or affected by His emotions but is rooted in His sovereign will and omnipotent love.

God promised:

> *My **mercy** I will keep for him forever,*
> *And My covenant shall stand firm with him.*
> *His seed also I will make to endure forever,*
> *And his throne as the days of heaven.*
>
> *"If his sons forsake My law*
> *And do not walk in My judgments,*
> *If they break My statutes*
> *And do not keep My commandments,*
> *Then I will punish their transgression with the rod,*
> *And their iniquity with stripes.*
> *Nevertheless My **lovingkindness** I will not utterly take from him,*
> *Nor allow My **faithfulness** to fail.* (Psalm 89:28–33) [24]

Joanie's Jewels

I never thought much about being Jewish; it was just part of my identity and culture. But my being Jewish did matter to other people. My family couldn't live in certain areas, I couldn't go to the school I wanted, join the club, or have the job that I wanted.

My perception of being Jewish changed when I became a follower of Jesus and read the Bible; I began to consider what it meant to be Jewish from God's perspective.

Furthermore I couldn't escape God's promise to bring the Jewish people back to the land of Israel. [25]

It wasn't long before He made it clear to me that I had go; I had to obey.

Moving to Israel changed my–well it changed everything. It was in this land that I finally understood the unique relationship God has with Israel. It was here that I understood and embraced what it means to be Jewish: the privilege, the purpose, and my personal responsibility.

Being Jewish, a believer in Christ, and an Israeli, I am living proof of God's covenant-keeping love. Israel is a restored nation, and the number of Jewish people believing in Jesus is increasing daily.

The apostle Paul says that when we look at Israel, we are seeing "life after death" (Romans 11:15).

God's *hesed* of Israel is further evidenced by His constant wooing, protecting, and providing for her.

Beloved this is not a political statement but a spiritual reality. So when people talk about the "problem of Israel," remind them it's not a political issue, but a spiritual one. And no one can solve a spiritual issue with a political solution!

Truth

Do you know that you speak Hebrew? Every time you say "amen" you are speaking Hebrew!

The root is אָמַן [*'aman*], which means *to confirm, support, uphold, to be established, be faithful.* [26]

We end our prayers with this precious word as an exclamation point. In doing so, we're saying, "It is so!" In other words, we are affirming that it is truth.

Derivatives of אָמַן [*aman*] used in Scripture include אֱמֶת [*'emet*], which is translated as *truth;* and אֱמוּנָה [*'emuna*], which is translated as *faith* and *faithful.*

All of these words carry the meaning of *certainty, solidarity, firmness regardless of circumstance, constant, or consistent.* Each evokes the picture of the strong arms of a parent holding a helpless infant. [27]

> *"Then I said to you, 'Do not be terrified, or afraid of them. The Lord your God, who goes before you, He will fight for you, according to all He did for you in Egypt before your eyes, and in the wilderness where you saw how the Lord your God carried you, as a man carries his son, in all the way that you went until you came to this place.'"* (Deuteronomy 1:29-31)

> *"The eternal God is your refuge,*
> *And underneath are the everlasting arms;*
> *He will thrust out the enemy from before you,*
> *And will say, 'Destroy!'"* (Deuteronomy 33:27)

Truth is not relative or personal. You can't have one truth and I have a different truth. Pilate asked Jesus, "What is truth?" (John 18:38). Jesus had already answered.

> *Jesus said to him, "I am the way, the truth, and the life."* (John 14:6a)

Joanie's Jewel

My faith in Jesus increased my knowledge and understanding of God's character.

And the Word became flesh and dwelt among us, and we beheld His glory, the glory as of the only begotten of the Father, full of grace and truth. (John 1:14)

As a result of my growing understanding of God, I discovered that who He is made a difference in my understanding of who I am!

In the past I defined and described myself through the eyes of others. But actually I was defining myself according to my perception of their perception of me.

Confusing? Yes!

Accurate? No!

Much of my identity was based on lies, lies that caused great pain and suffering. Jesus promises so much more. Jesus promises healing and freedom that comes from knowing the truth! It is truth that is based on who God is and who He made me to be through faith in Jesus.

"And you shall know the truth, and the truth shall make you free." (John 8:32)

"Therefore if the Son makes you free, you shall be free indeed." (John 8:36)

So many people today, especially younger generations, are seeking identity, a place to belong, and purpose for their lives. If their search does not end in faith in Jesus, their search will be useless.

Goodness and Truth Together

Now let's put these words together: וֶאֱמֶת חֶסֶד [*emet v'chesed*].

This expression, which appears many times throughout the Hebrew Bible, is extremely important.

Recognizing and understanding the contexts and consistent use of this phrase confronts and corrects the horrible distortion that God in the Old Testament is different from God in the New Testament. God is One, and His name (character) is one.

Let's look again at the passage in which God reveals the first part of His character with each of the self-revealing Hebrew words we've examined so far:

> And the LORD passed before him and proclaimed, "The LORD, the LORD God, **merciful** *(rachum) and* **gracious** *(chanun)*, **longsuffering** *('arek af), and abounding in* **goodness and truth** *('emet v'chesed)."* (Exodus 34:6–7a)

Hopefully you saw and heard those last words as a unit. The God of Mt. Sinai describes Himself as being "abounding in goodness and truth." If we were to change the NKJ translation by using a synonym for *hesed,* we would have "abounding in grace and truth."

Yes, you heard correctly. This set of words is the same description the apostle John uses for Jesus.

> For the law was given through Moses, but grace and truth came through Jesus Christ. (John 1:17)

In fact, the modern Hebrew translation of the New Testament uses the word *hesed* in this verse!

So pause for a moment and consider what is being contrasted in this passage. Most people say, "It is law versus grace and truth."

But if God never changes, then the God of Mount Sinai is the God of Calvary. The God of Mount Sinai is not a God of anger, war, and law and in contrast the God of Calvary a God of grace, mercy, and love.

If the comparison is NOT law versus grace and truth, what is it then?

It is the *method of mediation*.

God used Moses as a mediator between Israel and Himself. The law was written on tablets of stone and *given* to Moses, who in turn gave the tablets of the law to Israel.

But a better plan was already in place for the future, a better method of mediation. Jesus would be the better mediator. He *became* law as well as grace and truth. As the prophet Jeremiah foretold, there would come a time when God would make a new covenant with "the house of Israel and the house of Judah" (Jeremiah 31:31–33).

Now look at a verse I quoted earlier and see *'emet v'hesed* used together.

> *"My* **lovingkindness** *I will not utterly take from him,*
> *Nor allow My* **faithfulness** *to fail."* (Psalm 89:33)

Joanie's Jewel

Beloved, even this most rudimentary recognition of the Hebrew words has opened the Bible to me. As I read I look for the words *truth* and *faithfulness*, *mercy*, or *lovingkindness* when they come in a passage. They might be slightly separated, but they form a single thought.

Look with me at some passages where the phrase *'emet v'chesed* is used.

> *He will again have compassion on us,*
> *And will subdue our iniquities.*
> *You will cast all our sins*
> *Into the depths of the sea.*
> *You will give* **truth** *to Jacob*

And **mercy** *to Abraham,*
Which You have sworn to our fathers from days of old. (Micah 7:19–20)

Your **mercy**, *O* Lord, *is in the heavens;*
Your **faithfulness** *reaches to the clouds.* (Psalm 36:5)

Do not withhold Your tender mercies from me, O Lord;
Let Your **lovingkindness** *and Your* **truth** *continually preserve me.*
(Psalm 40:11)

Not unto us, O Lord, *not unto us,*
But to Your name give glory,
Because of Your **mercy**,
Because of Your **truth**. (Psalm 115:1)

And praise Your name
For Your **lovingkindness** *and Your* **truth**
For You have magnified Your word above all Your name. (Psalm 138:2)

And here is the ultimate:

Now I saw heaven opened, and behold, a white horse. And He who
sat on him was called **Faithful and True**, *and in righteousness He*
judges and makes war. (Revelation 19:11)

Beloved, what these passages reveal confronts and corrects the lie that the God of the Old Testament is different from the God of the New Testament.

I AM of the Old Testament is the same in
character and essence of Jesus in the New Testament.

Maybe we should all rip out the page in our Bible that separates the "Old" from the "New." It's one book!

Compassion

Although not in God's self-revelation in Exodus 34:5–7a, the word *compassion* must be considered as part of God's character. I include it here because Scripture often uses it interchangeably with "merciful" [*rachum*], the first word we studied (see: God Answers, Merciful).

The Hebrew word חָמַל [*chamal*] is defined as *to spare, have compassion, be responsible for.* [28]

"This word connotes the emotional response that results (or may result) in action to remove its object (and/or subject) from impending difficulty." [29]

Since we are all made in the image of God, it is not surprising that we often reveal glimpses of His compassion through our lives. The more we know Him and are transformed into His image, the more like Him we become.

Pharaoh's daughter showed *chamal* when she drew Moses out of the water.

> *Then the daughter of Pharaoh came down to bathe at the river. And her maidens walked along the riverside; and when she saw the ark among the reeds, she sent her maid to get it. And when she opened it, she saw the child, and behold, the baby wept. So she had* **compassion** *on him, and said, "This is one of the Hebrews' children."* (Exodus 2:5–6) [30]

Joanie's Jewel

Sometimes showing compassion takes just one simple act of kindness to someone else; other times it takes a substantial commitment. I am forever indebted to a friend who showed such compassion to me.

For reasons the medical world couldn't diagnose, I was without a voice for almost one and one-half years. In the beginning I could make a slight sound, but over the months I lived in an isolated world of complete silence.

My life revolves around speaking with people, making new acquaintances, and visiting good friends over a cup of coffee. So not having a voice was awful! Companionship as I knew it was gone.

Thankfully I had choices. I could "speak" through emails and Facebook. Or I could get together with others and use writing and reading to communicate. I would write, and they would read.

Admittedly I'd always scoffed at the compassion this particular friend had for stray cats. But she stood by me with that same compassion during those long, quiet months. Wow, did we celebrate when we could have a full conversation over the phone!

Exodus 34:7b

And now we move on to the second part of God's self-revelation found in the last portion of the Exodus 34:5–7 passage.

God had just said that He abounded in goodness and truth *'emet v'hesed,* yet immediately He repeats the word *hesed.* Let's look at the complete passage.

> *Now the LORD descended in the cloud and stood with him there, and proclaimed the name of the LORD. And the LORD passed before him and proclaimed, "The LORD, the LORD God, merciful and gracious, longsuffering, and abounding in* **goodness** *and truth, keeping* **mercy** *for thousands, forgiving iniquity and transgression and sin, by no means clearing the guilty, visiting the iniquity of the fathers upon the children and the children's children to the third and the fourth generation."* (Exodus 34:5–7)

Why do you think God chose to make this repetition?

I believe God is saying that while He abounds in goodness and truth, *'emet v'hesed*, He emphasizes His *hesed*, His covenant-keeping love.

Perhaps He knew that some people would prefer to describe Him using only the words *mercy, grace, lovingkindness, compassion,* and *longsuffering.* Others would ignore those attributes, choosing to condemn God as judgmental and cruel.

What's important, however, is what God says about Himself. He says that He "abounds," especially in *hesed*, covenant-keeping love.

The next word in God's self-revelation, *forgiving*, conjoins both aspects of God's character.

Forgiving

God's self-revelation includes His forgiveness as an aspect of His *hesed*.

> *[The* Lord *God]…keeping* **mercy** *for thousands,* **forgiving** *iniquity and transgression and sin…*(Exodus 34:7b)

The Hebrew root of *forgive* is נָשָׂא [*nasa'*], which is primarily defined as *to lift, carry, take.* [31]

Hence, the biblical concept of forgiveness is lifting up and carrying away our sins *and* bringing them to the cross on the back of Jesus.

In other words, God's love is not love and God's grace is not grace without God's forgiveness.

Joanie's Jewel

Until I became a follower of Jesus, forgiveness was only something I prayed for during Yom Kippur services. I really didn't recognize my desperate need for God's grace, mercy, and forgiveness.

Many Israelis are equally as spiritually blind and unaware.

The Hebrew word for forgiveness *nasa'* is not used today in Israel. Instead people use "*slicha*" for both "excuse me" and "I'm sorry" as the way to ask for forgiveness.

Many times we may say, "I'm sorry," but sometimes when we say it, we're not sorry at all. Other times we say those words when we really have nothing to be sorry for but do so as an effort to be polite.

As a result of these misuses, the response that is elicited is often a casual, "*En baya*," which means *no problem!* Consequently, forgiveness isn't a concept readily understood.

I was stunned, therefore, when I heard an Israeli tour guide say repeatedly, "I'm sorry," because he had nothing to be sorry for.

I had made an appointment for this man to create a special tour for some friends and me. We were very excited and eager, so when he called late the night before, I was concerned.

"Joanie, I'm so sorry. I was hit by a car today and cannot guide you tomorrow. But I tried to reach my friends to take you on the tour. I'm so very sorry."

He had been hit by a car and was in a lot of pain, yet he was sorry that he had to cancel the appointment!

His response challenged me greatly. I was concerned about his pain, but he was more concerned about being forgiven. Then I realized the probable cause of his desperation was he had never known the forgiveness of God or the forgiveness of others.

Even though saying "*slicha*" is considered sufficient in Israel, we *do* need to say we are sorry to God because with Him *there is* a problem!

God tells us the problem: iniquity, transgression, and sin, the words used in Exodus 34:7b.

Praise God that His love and forgiveness are abundantly available to all who ask. He never has and never will turn away the broken, the needy, or the helpless who come to Him through faith in Jesus' atoning sacrifice. Everyone, including the Egyptians in the Exodus story, were offered protection by anointing their doorposts with the blood of a lamb.

The apostle John was given a revelation of the glorified Jesus.

> *And I looked, and behold, in the midst of the throne and of the four living creatures, and in the midst of the elders, stood a Lamb as though it had been slain.* (Revelation 5:6) [32]

Iniquity

Iniquity is the first word God uses in Exodus 34:7b to describe specifically what He forgives.

The root of the Hebrew word עָוֹן [*'avon*] means "to bend or twist." This derivative expands that meaning to "the derived, abstract theological notion of the root: *infraction, crooked behavior, perversion, iniquity*." [33]

To understand this word and why we need God's forgiveness for iniquity, we have to accept that He has standards. Any deviation from those standards is iniquity.

Sadly today there is an aversion to the concept of God's standards, absolute truth, or morality. Ironically this aversion is in itself iniquity.

If people were honest, they would admit that all humanity instinctively knows there is a standard of morality and truth. Regardless of how some want it to read or try to reinterpret simple words, the Bible is clear about what God considers deviations from His standard.

> *The acts of the sinful nature are obvious: sexual immorality, impurity and debauchery; idolatry and witchcraft; hatred, discord, jealousy, fits of rage, selfish ambition, dissensions, factions and envy; drunkenness, orgies, and the like.* (Galatians 5:19–21 NIV)

In John's heavenly revelation, God assured him that admission to heaven was not open to everyone. God refuses admission to:

> *The cowardly, unbelieving, abominable, murderers, sexually immoral, sorcerers, idolaters, and all liars.* (Revelation 21:8a)

Joanie's Jewel

Being of an "older" generation, I am constantly amazed at the extent and depth of perversion, *'avon*, all around. Behavior that was hidden or discussed only in whispers is now paraded down our main streets and has become the "law of the land."

As I speak to young people around the world, they argue with me that truth and morality are relative. They believe that each person can decide what he or she wants to declare is true or determine right and wrong.

Yet this argument fades when I ask about the Holocaust. "Are you telling me that the Holocaust, which systematically murdered six million Jews plus another six million people, was morally right? Obviously it was morally acceptable to some people because they accepted as *truth* that the Jewish people were no more than rats and vermin."

At this point, my young friends become uncomfortable or silent; some even retract their arguments against absolute truth and morality.

Transgression

The second word God uses to describe what He forgives is *transgression*. The Hebrew word פֶּשַׁע [*pesha'*] means *a rebellion, breach of relationship (covenant) with God, revolt against God's moral and righteous standard, casting off allegiance, which creates a gulf between man and God.*[34]

God is the highest authority, so by every transgression we are ultimately transgressing against Him. Adam's and Eve's desire to be like God was rebellion against His authority. They chose to change their alliance from God to Satan. They replaced God's righteous and moral standards with their own.

Joanie's Jewel

Most of us understand rebellion in the context of the parent-child relationship. It might be easier for us to understand transgression as rebellion against God when we think of ourselves as His children.

When I was a young girl, a television commercial captured the attitude that sometimes accompanies transgression. With a clenched fist, a stomp of the foot, and a toss of the head, the child said, "I'd rather do it myself!"

While I don't remember what the issue was or even the product, I remember those words vividly. I remember because that attitude described my life. I didn't care if my mother was right (and she usually was). I refused to do things her way. Sadly, my rebellion caused a breach in our relationship that continued for many years.

That breach was healed when I recognized, admitted my rebellion, and asked my mother to forgive me. She was astounded and soon her tears mixed with mine as years of pain melted away.

In the same way our Heavenly Father longs and waits for us to admit our rebellion against Him and ask for His forgiveness. How wonderful to know that because Jesus took the penalty for our transgression, He is ready and eager to forgive.

Sin

The third word God uses to describe what He forgives is *sin*. The Hebrew word חַטָּאת [*chatta'ah*] from the root [*chata'*] means *to miss the mark (standard), failure to meet expectations, to err, be mistaken, to miss or wander from the path of uprightness and honor, to do or go wrong, to wander from the law of God, violate God's law.* [35]

Sin also implies and assumes that God has an absolute standard. God considers sin to be *anything* less than that standard—*anything* less than 100 percent.

Recently a devout Jewish man told me, "What matters is what is in your heart. As long as you abstain from sinful behavior, it's okay to have impure thoughts and desires."

I challenged this precious man with this verse from God's word to Samuel about King Saul:

> *But the LORD said to Samuel, "Do not look at his appearance or at his physical stature, because I have refused him. For the LORD does not see as man sees; for man looks at the outward appearance, but the LORD looks at the heart." (1 Samuel 16:7)*

God doesn't just look at the outward appearance or even at the sincerity of our hearts; He looks at us and judges us by His standard—that is, His Word.

I continued the challenge to this man by quoting another verse:

Therefore the LORD *said:*

> *"These people draw near with their mouths*
> *And honor Me with their lips,*
> *But have removed their hearts far from Me,*
> *And their fear toward Me is taught by the commandment of men."*
> (Isaiah 29:13)

He was obviously challenged and uncomfortable but had to agree with me.

Jesus said that God seeks worship in "spirit and truth" (John 4:24). If we are not so worshipping God, then our sincerity doesn't matter; we're not worshipping God as He deserves and demands to be worshipped. If we are not worshipping the God of the Bible in the way that He has prescribed–by grace through faith in Christ Jesus–we are worshipping wrongly. In fact, we may be worshipping an idol–a god we have created in our own likeness!

Joanie's Jewel

Every year I accompanied my parents to the synagogue during the most holy of all the feasts of the Lord, Yom Kippur, Day of Atonement. When I was old enough, I joined the adults praying all day. We fasted and confessed our sins according to the prayer book. That prayer book listed every conceivable sin, so I was sure that I was covered. In fact, I knew I had committed every sin on the list.

I was really sincere. I prayed and prayed and prayed. But at the end of the twenty-four hours of fasting and "affliction of soul," [36] I left the synagogue wondering if my sins had been forgiven. I wondered if my prayers had been heard.

How God's heart must break at the determination of people to continue to worship and serve Him, even with sincerity, yet remain in their sin because they have not been reconciled to God through faith in Jesus. God simply cannot forgive sin in any other manner than the one He has provided.

> *Jesus said to him, "I am the way, the truth, and the life. No one comes to the Father except through Me."* (John 14:6)

It is easier to be "a little pregnant" than to please God, ask Him to bless us, or to experience the fullness of His love while we remain in sin.

Visit

Now that we have seen the love and the grace of God, which constantly extends the opportunity for a loving relationship, we must consider God's justice. We see through the Passover story, there comes a time when His patience is over—when His nose finally becomes red. Because of the continued stubborn refusal of Pharaoh, God's anger "visited" through the plagues to punish all of Egypt (Exodus 7–11).

Notice God's justice as He describes Himself in the final portion of Exodus 34:5–7.

> *[The Lord God]…by no means clearing the guilty, visiting the iniquity of the fathers upon the children and the children's children to the third and the fourth generation.* (Exodus 34:7b)

As God's love compels Him to act, so does His justice. What does God do when we don't admit our sins and ask for forgiveness? He visits us.

The Hebrew word פָּקַד [*paqad*] means *to number, visit, punish, to attend to, muster, reckon after, care for, to pay attention to, observe, to pass in review, be called to account.* [37]

The word is used in many ways. Most often in the Torah and history books of Scripture, the word is used as "oversight" or "to number." [38]

In some instances, God's *paqad* was a blessing,[39] but as Israel spiraled deeper and deeper into sin, God warned of His "visit," or His judgment. [40]

> *"Behold, the days are coming," says the* Lord, *"that I will* **punish** *all who are circumcised with the uncircumcised—Egypt, Judah, Edom, the people of Ammon, Moab, and all who are in the farthest corners, who dwell in the wilderness. For all these nations are uncircumcised, and all the house of Israel are uncircumcised in the heart."* (Jeremiah 9:25–26)

We can't ignore the more troubling words at the end of the passage of God's self-revelation, the final portion of verse 7, God's punishing the children for the sins of the fathers.

> *…visiting the iniquity of the fathers upon the children and the children's children to the third and the fourth generation.* (Exodus 34:7b)

God warned Israel of the potential that the sins of the fathers would be passed down to their descendants.

> *The word of the* Lord *came to me again, saying, "What do you mean when you use this proverb concerning the land of Israel, saying:*
>
> *'The fathers have eaten sour grapes, and the children's teeth are set on edge'?"* (Ezekiel 18:1–2)

Even today it is not unusual to see troubling similarities in the lives of parents and the lives of their children. Counseling offices are filled with clients trying to blame their unacceptable behavior on their families, saying, "I'm just like my father (or mother)."

I can hear some of you say, "But that's not fair." Perhaps it's not fair according to today's humanistic culture where mankind is the center of the universe.

But in fact, God said there would come a day when every man, woman, and child would be judged individually.

> "As I live," says the LORD GOD, "you shall no longer use this proverb in Israel.
>
> > Behold, all souls are Mine;
> > The soul of the father
> > As well as the soul of the son is Mine;
> > The soul who sins shall die."
>
> "The soul who sins shall die. The son shall not bear the guilt of the father, nor the father bear the guilt of the son. The righteousness of the righteous shall be upon himself, and the wickedness of the wicked shall be upon himself." (Ezekiel 18:3–4, 20)

We might object or ignore the warning, but one day we will all pass before God Most High for a thorough inspection. At that time, He will pay close attention, and each of us will be called to account for all we have done in our lives, without regard to the sins of others.

God's *justice* demands that He "visit" with punishment the one who sins, whether father or son, mother or daughter. But God's *hesed* provides shelter and forgiveness. These two sides of God's character, love and justice, meet in the person of Jesus.

— 5 —

So What?

It's a Journey

Let's return to where we began, with the questions we want to ask God: "Why?" and "Who are You?"

To seek an explanation for why God does what He does is useless, achieving nothing but frustration.

> *"For My thoughts are not your thoughts,*
> *Nor are your ways My ways," says the LORD.*
> *"For as the heavens are higher than the earth,*
> *So are My ways higher than your ways,*
> *And My thoughts than your thoughts."* (Isaiah 55:8–9)

The better question is to ask what Moses asked, "Who are you?"

God answered Moses' question and the answer was sufficient for him to lead Israel through the wilderness. Even later when God told Moses he would not enter into the Promised Land, Moses didn't ask "Why?" Moses knew God.

From the time Adam and Eve walked with God in the Garden of Eden, God's desire has been to make Himself known to all who seek Him.

Everything He has done, from the creation of the world to the incarnation of Jesus, has been for a single purpose: to fill the earth with the knowledge, *yada'*, of His glory so that all people would know Him.[41]

Knowing God is a process as God slowly reveals Himself differently to each of us.

God started His relationship with Moses by introducing Himself as I AM, the God who is intimately and actively involved in the lives of His people.

But it took Moses the rest of his life to really know Him.

Getting to know God is a journey full of twists and turns, mountain peaks and valleys. We love to remember the mountain peaks, but generally it's when we're in the valley that we really get to know Him.

Joanie's Jewel

Sometimes we experience "coincidences" that can't be explained but stand out as road signs on the journey to knowing God.

In the very early days of my journey, He revealed Himself through what cannot be called "a coincidence."

The date was July 31, 1986. If I hadn't recorded it in my journal, it would have been easy to forget the date but not the memory of God's intimate and active involvement in my life. Only God could have orchestrated the details to bring my friend Dino to the same red light.

The fact that this was before we all had cell phones is what makes this story so amazing.

Here's what happened.

I was on my way to the dentist, an appointment I dreaded. The deal I'd arranged in advance was that *if* Dino would drive me to his house where

I could "sleep it off," the dentist would give me something to "relax" me during the procedure.

After I was well into the drive, I realized that I had left Dino's phone number on my desk back at the office. Dino was unreachable. I had no other option than to pray.

In a maze of traffic, confusion grew to concern and prayers morphed into groans. Well, what happened next might not seem like such a big deal, but add in these facts:

- I had driven on four major highways,
- Through five Los Angles communities,
- During rush hour traffic.

Yet as I pulled off at the final exit, Dino drove up right behind me!

It wasn't just a nice surprise. Dino being at that spot at that time was an answer to my prayer.

- God *heard* my groans.
- God *remembered* His covenant.
- God *looked* upon me.
- God *understood* my situation.
- SO God came to my rescue.

Since that day, whenever I am tempted to question God, I remember seeing Dino pull up to that red light. Sure there have been times of confusion, concern, or even frustration, but there has never been any doubt. I know God, and I know that He hears and answers when I call out to Him.

So I have several questions for you, beloved reader.

Questions for You

Beloved, do you want to know God?

This might seem like a strange question to ask, especially if you're reading this book. But it's really not such a strange question. Some people just don't want to know God or even admit that God exists.

Sarah (not her real name) is a precious Israeli woman and a cherished friend. Early in our friendship she told me her amazing story of being completely cured of bone cancer.

The cancer had been quite painful and very aggressive. All the doctors called it a miracle. But not Sarah.

"I don't want to believe in God, so I will not call this a miracle," she said.

Of course I was astounded. "Why refuse to even consider that God exists?"

"Because," she explained, "if I admit that there is a God and admit that He healed me, then I'd have to believe and trust Him with the rest of my life. So no, I don't want to know Him!"

Do you feel the same as Sarah? Or perhaps you've already made a covenant with God. So my second question for you is, "Do you want to know Him better?"

— 6 —

The Choice is Yours

In the final hours of his life, Moses challenged Israel to make a decision.

> *"I call heaven and earth as witnesses today against you, that I have set before you life and death, blessing and cursing; therefore choose life, that both you and your descendants may live."* (Deuteronomy 30:19)

You see, Beloved, while Israel was in slavery the people knew God only through the stories passed down to them from their ancestors. But then they saw His mighty acts to rescue them from Egypt. Yet when they had the opportunity to come closer, they were afraid.

> *Now all the people witnessed the thunderings, the lightning flashes, the sound of the trumpet, and the mountain smoking; and when the people saw it, they trembled and stood afar off. Then they said to Moses, "You speak with us, and we will hear; but let not God speak with us, lest we die."*
>
> *And Moses said to the people, "Do not fear; for God has come to test you, and that His fear may be before you, so that you may not sin." So the people stood afar off, but Moses drew near the thick darkness where God was.* (Exodus 20:18–21)

Moses knew that Israel's limited knowledge of God would not be enough to keep the people from fear and continued rebellion as they followed His lead through the desert.

Israel had to make a decision; they had to choose.

Beloved, God is giving you the same opportunity. What will you choose? How will you answer?

Do you want to know God?

Recently I told an Israeli that I was writing this book about knowing God. He laughed at me saying, "No one can know God."

He was wrong.

Beloved, you can have a personal and intimate relationship with the God of the universe through faith in Jesus, Yeshua the Messiah.

Perhaps you have also experienced the pain of rejection, abandonment, and betrayal. As a result, you might be cautious about trusting God.

It is my prayer that these words of Jesus will pierce the pain and bring hope and peace to your heart:

> *"Come to Me, all you who labor and are heavy laden, and I will give you rest. Take My yoke upon you and learn from Me, for I am gentle and lowly in heart, and you will find rest for your souls. For My yoke is easy and My burden is light."* (Matthew 11:28–30)

> *"All that the Father gives Me will come to Me, and the one who comes to Me I will by no means cast out."* (John 6:37)

> *"[And] I give them eternal life, and they shall never perish; neither shall anyone snatch them out of My hand."* (John 10:28)

Beloved of God, Jesus is extending His nail-pierced hand to you to deliver you from the bondage of sin, sorrow, and sickness.

He carried you, your past, present, and future on His back to the cross. But to have a relationship, you must be reconciled to God, which can only happen by God's grace through your faith in Jesus' sacrifice.

Remember I said that I didn't understand the "Why?" of the cross? When I recognized my sin, I understood and had my answer; Jesus accepted the punishment I deserved.

You see, God's law says that there must be a sacrifice to pay the penalty for sin. Jesus paid that penalty for me and for you by His sacrifice.

So once I had the answer to "Why?" I repented. Repentance is more than being sorry for past sin; it is to make a determined decision to turn away from any and all present and future sin. My repentance resulted in my being forgiven and being reconciled to God.

> *If we confess our sins, He is faithful and just to forgive us our sins and to cleanse us from all unrighteousness.* (1 John 1:9)

So here are several things important for you to understand:

- Regardless of your attempts to be good, you will never be good enough. The Bible says that we are all born in and remain in bondage to sin. As we saw before, it is that sin that makes the impassable separation between you and God.
- The first step in being reconciled to God (entering into a relationship) is recognizing and admitting that you are bound in sin. You are not simply someone who "happens" to sin occasionally; your very nature is prone to sin. That's what *confession* means, agreeing with God.
- The second step is to repent. Repentance is more than just feeling sad; it means feeling so bad and guilty that you determine NOT to sin. In other words, it means turning away, going in the opposite direction from sin.

- The third step is believing in Jesus as Savior, the only way to have a personal relationship with God. As I said above, it is His sacrifice that enables you to be reconciled to God.

When you confess, repent, embrace Jesus as Savior, and commit your life to God, you become a new creation. You are given a new and sinless heart, filled with God's Holy Spirit.

To grow in knowledge of His grace and wisdom and become the person He created you to be, you must completely trust His love and surrender to His will. Doing so is a continual process that allows Him to lead you into a life that will bring you the most satisfaction and fruitfulness.

Then your name will be written in the Lamb's Book of Life for all eternity, and nothing will separate you from His love (Revelation 3:5).

Jesus has made the way for you, and now it is up to you to take the next step. I invite you to consider praying the prayer of salvation below.

Prayer of Salvation

Father in Heaven, I confess that I have lived a life of selfishness and sin, and I ask You now to forgive me of all that I have done: sins that I remember and those I have forgotten. Forgive my sin of actions as well as of thoughts. I choose to believe in Jesus as the only way of forgiveness, cleansing, and salvation. I give You my heart and my life.

Thank You for loving me, forgiving me, and revealing Yourself to me.

With Your help, through the Holy Spirit, I will follow and obey You all the days of my life. Thank You for Your promise to never leave or forsake me. In Jesus' name I pray. Amen!

Do you want to know God better?

Sometimes choices are simple but not easy to make. Making this choice is like that—simple but not easy.

Joanie's Jewel

One day in prayer I had the overwhelming, almost desperate desire to know God more intimately. I felt as though I were standing on the edge of a dark forest and God was very far away.

As I began to cry, the Holy Spirit seemed to whisper to my innermost being.

"Come closer."

"But it's dark, and I cannot see anything. I'm afraid," I confessed.

"That's exactly why you feel so far from Me. You are afraid to walk in complete surrender and trust. You must let go of trying to control and trust My love for you."

I knew at that moment I had to make a choice.

The Bible tells us that because of the intensity of His light, mortal men cannot view God's glory. Yet He is surrounded by darkness, thunder, and lightning (Psalms 18:8–10; 97:2).

The choice was simple, but it was not easy.

I stepped into the darkness.

Knowing and following God is the only way to a purposeful and abundant life in this world and eternal life thereafter. Yes, the choice to walk into the darkness was simple.

Although my journey with God has not always been easy, it has been and will always be worth it.

Perhaps you have already made the step of faith, but life with its challenges and pressures have gotten in the way of you knowing God more and more. If so, I invite you to make a recommitment to your initial prayer of salvation and decision to follow Jesus using the prayer that follows or something similar.

Prayer of Recommitment

My Father, thank You for Your faithful love. You were faithful when I was not. I confess that I have wandered far away from You, sometimes by my thoughts and sometimes by my actions. I have tried to be in control of my life, and it hasn't worked! You are God, and I am not. I need You, Father. I don't want to live another minute without Your sweet Presence. Please forgive me of my sins and even my neglect when I've put people or things ahead of You.

Help me, Holy Spirit, to know the Father's love. Fill me again with the sense of Your peace, Your love, and Your joy.

Jesus, I give You my hand, my heart, and my life. Thank you for Your abundant forgiveness and grace through my faith in Jesus. I am Yours, and You are mine.

In Your name, Jesus, I pray. Amen.

— 7 —

An Affectionate Shalom

As we come to the end of this journey to know who God is, I pray that our time together has been a blessing. Perhaps God has used something in these pages to challenge, to heal, or even to change your life.

Writing this has been a blessing for me. God has challenged, healed, and impacted my life. Remembering these special "jewels" of my life has renewed my passion to know Him better.

All our lives are filled with jewels, gifts from God so we will know Him. Just look around and you will see jewels from the Word, jewels from your life, and jewels from the lives of others.

Please share them with me.

So I bid you "Shalom and blessings from Jerusalem."

With love,

Joanie

ENDNOTES

1. God changed the names of Sarah, Jacob, and even Simon Peter: Genesis 17:15; 32:28; Matthew 16:18.

2. R. Harris Laird, Gleason L. Archer Jr., and Bruce K. Waltke, *Theological Wordbook of the Old Testament* (TWOT) (Chicago: Moody Press, 2003), 491, #491.

   God gives His memorial name to Moses (Exodus 3:14) as: אֶהְיֶה [*ehyeh*], which means "to be." The English YHWH is usually pronounced today as *Yah-veh* or *Yah-ho-vah* or simply *yod, hey, vav, hey*, which are the Hebrew letters. However, Hebrew speakers hear something very profound. With a bit of manipulating the letters, they hear the verb in the past הָיָה [*hayah*], the present הֹוֶה [*hoveh*], and the future יהיה [*ihiyeh*].

3. Francis Brown, S. R. Driver, Charles A. Briggs, *The New Brown-Driver-Briggs-Gesenius Hebrew and English Lexicon* (BDB) (Peabody, MA: Hendrickson, 1979), 1033, #8085.

4. See also: 1 Chronicles 16:7–36; Nehemiah 1:5; Psalm 105; Daniel 9:3–4.

5. Laird, TWOT, 823, #2095.

   H7200 - ra'ah – Strong's Hebrew Lexicon (KJV). Blue Letter Bible. Accessed 4 Jun, 2016. https://www.blueletterbible.org//lang/lexicon/lexicon.cfm?Strongs=H7200&t=KJV.

6. Genesis 16:10–12.

7. See: http://novea.org, "Witness to Israel."

8. Laird, TWOT, 366, #848.

   H3045 - yada` - Strong's Hebrew Lexicon (KJV). Blue Letter Bible. Accessed 4 Jun, 2016. https://www.blueletterbible.org//lang/lexicon/lexicon.cfm?Strongs=H3045&t=KJV.

9. To read my full testimony see: www.novea.org

10. See also: Exodus 20:2; Leviticus 25:38; Numbers 15:41; 1 Chronicles 17:21; Micah 6:4; Amos 2:10.

11. See also: Psalms 115:12; 116:1, 5; 118.

12. Probably all Christians know John 3:16, but few understand the context. Knowing context is a principle of Bible study; knowing John 3:9–17 is significant to knowing the character of God.

> Although John 3:16 is often used in evangelistic messages, Jesus was not talking to an unbeliever but THE teacher in Israel. Nicodemus was well versed in the Hebrew Bible and would have been very familiar with the reference to the bronze serpent.
>
> > Numbers 21:4–9 recounts God's response to Israel's complaint about His provision. He sent "fiery snakes" whose bites were fatal. The people finally repented. But instead of taking away the snakes, God made a provision to escape from death.
> >
> > *Then the LORD said to Moses, "Make a fiery serpent, and set it on a pole; and it shall be that everyone who is bitten, when he looks at it, shall live." (Numbers 21:8)*
> >
> > This incident in Israel's history foreshadowed the New Covenant. More than that it showed the immutability of God's character.
> >
> > - God's holiness cannot tolerate sin and will punish (visit) the one who sins.
> > - God hears the groaning of the people who are in bondage to sin (their repentance).
> > - God acts by providing a way of escape from death (substitutionary sacrifice).
> > - Reconciliation requires faith and obedience.
> > - God remains faithful to the covenant made by His grace though faith.
> >
> > Jesus' words were very precise. Today we often quote Him as saying, "You must believe THAT…" But that's not what He said; it's not what is required. Reconciliation with God requires that a person believes IN Jesus, believes IN the efficacy and sufficiency of Christ's atonement.

Furthermore, the Greek grammar is better translated as, "Whoever believes and **keeps on believing in Him**." Faith is more than a single decision in one point of time, but a lifetime of determined decisions.

So the significance of knowing the context of John 3:16 is the truth of God's immutable character. The God of Mt. Sinai is the same as the God of Calvary.

13. Isaac Watts, "When I Survey the Wondrous Cross," *Hymns Ancient and Modern* (London, William Clowes and Sons Ltd. 1924) #108.

14. Joan Lipis, *Celebrate Jesus!* (Keller, TX, Palm Tree Productions, 2009) 267–268.

15. See also: Nehemiah 9:17b; Psalm 103:8; Joel 2:13; Jonah 4:2.

16. L. Koehler & W. Baumgartner, eds. (1999), *The Hebrew and Aramaic Lexicon of the Old Testament* (HALOT) [Electronic form], (Leiden, Netherlands: Brill.), #8747.

17. Laird, TWOT, 841, #2146a.

18. Brown, BDB, 335–336, #2603.

19. "In Jesus' teaching the concept of grace in the sense of the undeserved gift of God evidently did not occur. But the theme of his teaching and his acts as a whole centered on God's condescension to the weak, poor, hopeless, lost. For Paul χάρις [*charis*] is the essence of God's decisive saving act in Jesus Christ, which took place in his sacrificial death and all of its consequences in the present and future." Colin Brown, The New International Dictionary of New Testament Theology, (Grand Rapids: Zondervan Publishing House, 1976) 116-119.

20. Ibid. 58, #133a.

21. See also: Ruth 2:20; 3:10.

22. Loved: [*'ahab*]; grace: [*chanan*]; favor: [*chesed*].

23. See also: Nehemiah 9; Psalm 78; 89; Isaiah 1:18; 40:1–2; Hosea 2:19.

24. Mercy: [*chanan*]; unfailing love: [*chesed*]; compassion: [*rachum*].

25. See also: Psalm 126:1–4; Isaiah 11:11; Ezekiel 37:21–22; Jeremiah 27:22. For a more complete list of references, see: www.lunchtimeprayer.com, category, "Gathering and Return of the Jewish People."

26. Laird, TWOT, 51–53, #116.

27. Ibid.

28. Brown, BDB, 328, #2550.

29. Laird, TWOT, 296, #676.

30. Also Ezekiel 16:1–8; Ephesians 2:1–5.

31. Brown, BDB, 669, #5375.

32. When John the Baptizer described Jesus as the "Lamb of God who takes away the sin of the world!" he was conjoining the lamb of Passover and the sacrifice of Yom Kippur. The lamb of Passover protected all who would find refuge under its sacrificial blood but it did not affect sin. That was done through the blood of the sacrifice of Yom Kippur. John's audience was the Jews of Israel who would understand. Apostle John often called Jesus "the lamb." See also: John 1:29, 36; Revelation 14:10; 15:3.

33. Laird, TWOT, 650, #1577a.

34. Laird, TWOT, 741, #1846a.

35. J. Strong, (1996) *The Exhaustive Concordance of the Bible* [Electronic form], Ontario: Woodside Bible Fellowship. #2403

36. Leviticus 23:26.

37. Laird, TWOT, 731, #1802.

38. For "number" see: Exodus 30:12–14; Numbers 1:3; Joshua 8:10. For "oversight" see: Genesis 39:5; 1 Kings 11:28.

39. See Exodus 4:31; 1 Samuel 2:21.

40. See Isaiah 13:11; Jeremiah 5:29; 11:22; Hosea 2:13; 12:2; Amos 3:2, 4.

41. See also: Numbers 14:2; Isaiah 11:9; Habakkuk 2:14.

ADDITIONAL RESOURCES

My Favorite Resources for the Greek and Hebrew Interlinear Bible:
https://www.blueletterbible.org

For etymology of Classical Greek, LXX, and New Testament Greek:
Brown, Colin, ed. *The New International Dictionary of the New Testament*. Grand Rapids: Zondervan Publishing House, 1975.

For connotations of Hebrew words:
Harris, R. Laird, ed. *Theological Wordbook of the Old Testament*. Chicago: Moody Press, 1980.

KEEPING IN TOUCH

Email:

Novea@novea.org

Newsletter:

http://eepurl.com/bQaAAH

Websites:

www.novea.org

- Simcha blog: (Celebrating the Feasts of the Lord)
- Joanie's Jewels

www.lunchtimeprayer.com

You Tube:

Lunchtime Prayer for Israel

- Subscribe: https://www.youtube.com/channel/ UCE1cs4SLVgY3zHGadXXcJFQ

Novea Ministries

- Subscribe: https://www.youtube.com/channel/ UCBme4ZyxsZN6G6AgWkG0czw

BOOKS AND MEDIA BY JOANIE

Available through: www.novea.org/store

Celebrate Jesus!
Christian Perspective of the Feasts of the Lord

An easy to use resource giving the reader the biblical foundation and suggesting the personal application for each of the feasts. Good for pastors, educators and all who want to celebrate Jesus!

Celebrate Passover:
Three Tables Messianic Haggadah

The complete resource for your celebration of Passover. The liturgy takes you from the table of Moses in Egypt, to the table of Jesus in Jerusalem, and culminates at the banquet table of the Marriage Supper of the Lamb.

Celebrate God's Love:
Christmas/Hanukkah; Fact and Fiction

Confronts the myths and celebrates the truths of both holidays.

Celebrate the Lamb:
Messianic Perspective of Passover

Uses excerpts from *Celebrate Jesus!* yet corrects the English translations and expands the meanings of the Hebrew words for each holiday.

"Who Are You?" Moses asks God

Explores the words God uses to describe Himself through the original Hebrew and illustrations from Joanie's life.

Is God Through with Israel? Certainly Not!

A 90 day prayer guide based on Romans 9-11.

The Biblical Response to Israel (DVD)

Encourages those who love the God of Israel and His Messiah to partner with God's plans and purposes for Israel and the Jewish people.

Made in the USA
Columbia, SC
16 June 2019